Original title:
Deep Dive into Relationships

Copyright © 2024 Swan Charm
All rights reserved.

Author: Swan Charm
ISBN HARDBACK: 978-9916-86-677-1
ISBN PAPERBACK: 978-9916-86-678-8
ISBN EBOOK: 978-9916-86-679-5

Beneath the Waves of Time

In depths where silence weaves its spell,
The secrets of the past do dwell.
A whispering tide, a gentle sigh,
In watery realms where dreams float by.

Each bubble floats a story old,
Of sunken ships and treasures told.
With coral castles, great and grand,
Guarded by fish in a watery band.

The echoes of laughter blend with the sea,
Where shadows dance, wild and free.
Time drips slowly like falling sand,
Weaving memories in a timeless strand.

Beneath the waves, where time stands still,
A world concealed, a heart to fill.
Each current carries a distant song,
A melody of where we once belonged.

The moonlight glimmers on the crest,
Inviting all to take a rest.
In the cradle of tides, we all must find,
The beauty hidden, the ties that bind.

Depths of Vulnerability

In shadows deep, fears quietly dwell,
Each heartbeat whispers, secrets to tell.
Beneath the surface, a tempest may stir,
The strength in the softness, we often defer.

Unravel the layers, embrace what is true,
For courage is found in the scars that we rue.
A fragile touch, yet fiercely we stand,
In vulnerability's depths, we find our own hand.

The Labyrinth of Us

In twisted paths, we wander and roam,
Together we carve out a place called home.
With every turn, a lesson unfolds,
In the maze of our hearts, a love story told.

Through corridors dark, we seek out the light,
Each step hand in hand, we conquer the night.
For in every riddle, a thread we will trace,
The labyrinth of us, a sacred embrace.

Mysterious Tides of Affection

In stillness, the waves of feeling do rise,
Whispers of longing, beneath moonlit skies.
A rhythm that pulls us, like stars in the sea,
In the depths of our souls, we uncover what's free.

Each ebb and flow, a dance we create,
Lost in the currents, we navigate fate.
With every caress, the universe sighs,
Mysterious tides, where true love never lies.

Drenched in Connection

In the pouring rain, we find our embrace,
Drenched in connection, no fear of the chase.
With laughter like thunder, we rise and we fall,
Wrapped in the warmth of our love's endless call.

Underneath all storms, a spark we ignite,
Each droplet a promise, a future so bright.
In the rhythm of life, our hearts beat in time,
Drenched in connection, forever we'll climb.

Anchored in Hope

In stormy seas, we brace ourselves,
With dreams that gently guide us home.
Each wave a lesson, strong and bold,
We rise, though often we may roam.

The anchor holds in darkest nights,
A light that shines through shadows cast.
With whispered prayers, our spirits lift,
We find our peace, as storms depart.

The Currents of Belonging

In rivers wide, our hearts entwine,
Each ebb and flow a tale to share.
Together we navigate the tides,
In bonds unbroken, always there.

The gentle brush of hands held tight,
Across the distance, love will bridge.
In whispers soft, in laughter bright,
We carve our names on memory's edge.

Still Waters Run Deep

Beneath the calm, a world unfolds,
Where dreams and secrets gently sleep.
The surface glimmers, yet remains,
A hint that still waters run deep.

With quiet strength, we face the storms,
Reflecting skies of changing hue.
In solitude, we find our truth,
As whispers of the heart break through.

Falling Into Trust

In shadows cast by doubt and fear,
We take the leap, our courage found.
With every step, a heart draws near,
In faith, we rise from solid ground.

The dance of trust, both wild and free,
A journey shared, our souls laid bare.
In the embrace of vulnerability,
We find the strength to truly care.

The Undercurrent of Us

In the quiet spaces, we collide,
Where secrets linger, hearts abide.
A silent pact beneath the hue,
The tide of time, pulling me to you.

Whispers dance in shadows, soft and true,
In every glance, a world anew.
The currents call, we drift and sway,
Together bound, we'll find our way.

With every heartbeat, echoes sound,
A rhythm forged in what we've found.
In hidden depths, our spirits roam,
The undercurrent, our shared home.

Whispers in the Waves

Gentle rhythms kiss the shore,
Whispers carried, forevermore.
The ocean breathes, its secrets low,
In every swell, the stories flow.

Crashing laughter, salt on skin,
Moments captured, deep within.
The tide rushes, pulls us closer,
Lost in dreams, a silent poser.

Beyond the foam, where silence lies,
We paint our hopes beneath the skies.
Together drifting, hand in hand,
Whispers calling from the sand.

The Depths of Trust

In murky waters, shadows blend,
A fragile line, we learn to bend.
The depths we dive, with hearts laid bare,
In silent sighs, our souls declare.

Each glance a promise, soft and warm,
In storms we find our calm, our balm.
The currents swirl, but we hold tight,
Guided by love, through darkest night.

In every heartbeat, truth resides,
A lighthouse shining, where hope abides.
Together fearless, we break free,
In trust's embrace, we find the sea.

Threads Woven in Silence

In quiet moments, threads entwine,
A tapestry of thoughts divine.
Each whisper stitches layers tight,
In silent corners, hearts ignite.

With every gaze, a knot is formed,
In gentle silence, we're reborn.
The fabric hums, a melody sweet,
In woven dreams, our spirits meet.

Colors blend in shaded light,
The threads connect, our souls take flight.
In silence bold, we stand as one,
A masterpiece, when day is done.

Bridges Over Waves

Through misty air the bridges rise,
Connecting hearts beneath the skies.
Waves crash softly on the shore,
Whispers of dreams forevermore.

The tides may shift, the world may change,
Yet bonds of love will not estrange.
Each step taken on this path,
Brings us closer, warms the heart.

The sun will set, the night will fall,
But hope will guide us through it all.
Hand in hand, we face the fight,
Bridges gleaming in the night.

With every wave, a story told,
Tales of courage, brave and bold.
From shore to shore, we shall admire,
The bridges built through love's own fire.

In harmony, we dance and sway,
Together strong, we'll find our way.
Oceans wide cannot divide,
For in our hearts, we will abide.

When Souls Collide

In the chaos of a crowded room,
Two souls flicker, breaking gloom.
Like stars colliding in the night,
A spark ignites, a sudden light.

Words unspoken, yet understood,
In silent glances, hearts are good.
Time stands still in this embrace,
Two wanderers find their place.

Tangled fates and fortune's grace,
In destiny's dance, we find our space.
Echoes linger, soft and sweet,
A harmony that feels complete.

Through storms and trials, we've endured,
In every wound, love's truth secured.
When darkness falls, we'll hold the flame,
For together, we're never the same.

With every heartbeat, bonds expand,
A tapestry woven, hand in hand.
As souls collide, we rise above,
In this vast world, we find our love.

Beneath the Facade

Behind the smile, a story lies,
A tapestry of lows and highs.
Masks we wear with practiced grace,
Yet hearts ache in stillness, space.

In crowded rooms, we hide our fears,
The laughter often masks the tears.
Beneath the surface, shadows creep,
A secret world, a soul to keep.

But when the night embraces dark,
Truth unveils each hidden spark.
In whispered words, we find our voice,
In vulnerability, we make our choice.

The layers peel, exposing light,
In honest moments, we unite.
Together we'll face the stormy sea,
Beneath the facade, we can be free.

Let us embrace the scars we bear,
For in our truths, the love we share.
No more hiding, let souls entwine,
Beneath the facade, we brightly shine.

Ripples of Memories

In still waters, whispers flow,
Ripples of memories, soft and slow.
Time may fade, but echoes remain,
A gentle touch, a lingering pain.

Through twilight's hues, the past we trace,
In shadows that time cannot erase.
Each moment captured, a fleeting glance,
In the dance of fate, we take our chance.

Laughter and tears, intertwined,
In woven hearts, our stories bind.
Like leaves that fall and drift away,
Memories linger, in their play.

The gentle waves may shift the sand,
But love's embrace forever stands.
In every ripple, a tale to greet,
Remnants of love, both bitter and sweet.

So hold these moments close and dear,
For in the heart, they always steer.
As time flows on, let us believe,
In ripples of memories, we achieve.

Currents of Understanding

In whispers soft, the currents flow,
A river deep where feelings grow.
With every wave, truth's light we find,
A journey shared, two hearts aligned.

Beneath the surface, depths conceal,
The stories told that time reveals.
We navigate through storm and calm,
Embracing all, a soothing balm.

Through rocky paths and tranquil streams,
Together bound by shared hopes and dreams.
The current pulls, yet we are free,
In this vast sea of you and me.

Secrets Beneath the Skin

Beneath the skin, the stories hum,
In silent tones, where shadows come.
Each scar a tale, each mark a sign,
Of battles fought, of hearts divine.

In tender glances, secrets lye,
In every touch, whispers reply.
The warmth, the pulse, a dance so sweet,
Revealing truths, where souls do meet.

The layers peel, the heart exposed,
With every breath, new paths disclosed.
In vulnerability, we dare,
To share our fears, stripped bare.

Uncharted Waters of Affection

In uncharted waters, hearts set sail,
With every wave, new tales unveil.
The compass spins, yet we believe,
In love's embrace, we dare to weave.

The horizon beckons, vast and wide,
With hopes and dreams, we take the ride.
Each current pulls, yet steady we steer,
Through tempests wild, we hold what's dear.

The depths unknown, yet eyes aglow,
In silent promise, our spirits grow.
Together we navigate, bold and brave,
With every heartbeat, a love to save.

Chasing Shadows of Intimacy

In the twilight's glow, we chase the night,
Fleeting moments, soft and light.
In shadows cast, our spirits dance,
Whispers shared, a secret chance.

The world fades out, just you and I,
Where laughter rings and hearts comply.
In gentle touches, the lines blur,
As seconds linger, we start to stir.

Through fleeting glances, intimacy brews,
In every heartbeat, what's real construes.
Together we wander, hand in hand,
Chasing shadows in a twilight land.

Beneath the Surface

Whispers linger just below,
Secrets held in gentle flow.
Ripples dance on quiet streams,
Tales untold, in silent dreams.

Depths conceal what eyes can't see,
Hidden shapes, wild and free.
Flowing currents hide the truth,
Beneath the surface, lost in youth.

An echo calls from far away,
A beckoning to join the play.
Voices murmur in the night,
Drawing shadows into light.

Fragile bonds, like threads of gold,
Hold the moments, soft and bold.
Beneath the calm, a storm may brew,
Feelings deep, yet few pursue.

What lies within the quiet heart?
A world apart where dreams may start.
Beneath the surface, stillness waits,
For brave souls to open gates.

Echoes of Connection

In the silence, echoes blend,
Whispers that the heart can send.
Messages of love and light,
Travel through the endless night.

Threads of fate spin out their lies,
Tales of joy, and silent cries.
Connections weave both near and far,
Guiding us, like northern star.

Gentle touches, a fleeting glance,
Every heartbeat, a shared dance.
In the shadows, souls ignite,
Finding peace in shared twilight.

Waves of laughter, shadows play,
In moments that just slip away.
Glimmers spark in weary eyes,
Together finding shared skies.

Through the echoes, voices rise,
Unseen bonds that never die.
In connection, we find our way,
A tapestry through night and day.

Tides of Emotion

Waves crash softly on the shore,
Whispers of the heart's deep lore.
Rising tides, they pull and sway,
Emotions dance, then drift away.

Currents strong, yet soft embrace,
Tidal pools hold dreams to trace.
Flowing freely with the moon,
Carrying our love's sweet tune.

In the depths, the shadows roam,
Each sigh becomes a part of home.
With every surge, there comes a calm,
Hearts entwined like nature's psalm.

Drowning fears in silver tides,
Where hope and longing coincide.
Together, riding every swell,
In the depths, we know so well.

Just like water, life will flow,
Through the highs and deepest low.
Tides of emotion ebb and swell,
A journey shared, our sacred well.

Beneath the Facade

Masks we wear, they hide the pain,
Smiles adorn the hurt like rain.
Behind the laughs, a quiet plea,
Seeking truth to set us free.

Layers thick, yet fragile hearts,
Fearful of the pain it sparks.
Walls constructed, tough and strong,
But loneliness sings its song.

In every glance, a deeper story,
Yearning for a glimpse of glory.
In silence, truth begins to wake,
Beneath the facade, we all ache.

Fragile souls in bright disguise,
Searching for the clear blue skies.
In the shadows, secrets lie,
But hope remains, and will not die.

Together we can break the frame,
Embrace the flawed without the shame.
Beneath the facade, courage glows,
A bond that only the heart knows.

Finding Solid Ground

In the midst of swirling winds,
I search for resting place,
Among the chaos loud and wild,
I hope to find some grace.

Footsteps falter on the path,
Each step a whispered prayer,
In shadows long I tread with care,
Seeking solace in the air.

The earth beneath beckons me near,
With roots as firm as stone,
I anchor deep, I hold my ground,
And find I am not alone.

Fingers brush the cool, soft earth,
Life pulses in a beat,
A harmony of heart and soul,
In nature's dance, I meet.

So here I stand, with open arms,
Embracing all around,
In the beauty of this moment,
I finally feel profound.

Beneath the Weight of Words

Words tumble like a heavy load,
Crushed beneath their silent weight,
Each syllable a world alone,
Yet longing to communicate.

In spoken truths and whispered dreams,
We search for bonds so true,
Yet fear can twist the clearest lines,
And leave the heart askew.

A gaze can speak more than a word,
When silence fills the air,
Each moment swells with quiet thoughts,
That hearts might wish to share.

But we build walls, we hide away,
Afraid to let love show,
Beneath the weight of what we say,
The fear continues to grow.

If only we could shed the masks,
And let our true selves breathe,
We'd find in honest vulnerability,
The trust we both can weave.

The Rhythm of Connection

In the pulse of life, we find our way,
A cadence soft and sweet,
With every heart that beats as one,
Our souls begin to greet.

The laughter shared, the tears we shed,
A symphony of sound,
With harmony in every note,
Our love is truly found.

We dance to rhythms deep and true,
In moments caught in time,
Each step a movement toward the light,
In perfect, gentle rhyme.

Connection flows like water clear,
A river wide and free,
In currents strong, we dive within,
Together you and me.

And through the ebb and flow of life,
We find our anchor here,
In every beat, our hearts align,
Creating joy sincere.

Shores of Understanding

Waves crash upon the sandy shores,
Each crest a tale to tell,
As tides of time shift ever more,
In whispers of the swell.

With every grain that slips away,
We learn what truly lasts,
In moments shared between the shores,
The echoes of our pasts.

To walk the beach beneath the sun,
With hearts laid open wide,
Is to embrace the journey made,
Together side by side.

Finding beauty in the breaks,
And unity in the stride,
In every touch of salty air,
Our hearts become our guide.

Here on these shores of understanding,
We plant our dreams like seeds,
And watch as love takes root and grows,
In every heart that leads.

Cultivating Vulnerability

In the soil of secrets, we sow our fears,
Tender roots of trust, nourished by tears.
Braving the winds, we dance with our flaws,
Building the courage to bare our raw hearts.

Each breath a whisper, a softening grace,
Revealing the shadows, a delicate place.
Together we harvest what time has bestowed,
Finding the strength in the stories we've told.

Hands intertwined, we face the unknown,
Blossoming wild in the truth we have grown.
Fragile yet fierce, like the petals we share,
Embracing the moments, the weight of the air.

In this garden of souls, we learn to believe,
That vulnerability's light helps us retrieve.
With every heartbeat, we cultivate light,
For in our surrender, we find our true might.

Heartbeats in Harmony

In the symphony of silence, I hear your call,
A rhythm of comfort that cradles us all.
With every heartbeat, a pulse intertwines,
Two souls in sync, like the stars that align.

Through valleys of shadows and mountains of dreams,
We dance to the cadence of soft moonbeams.
Each laugh a note, each tear a refrain,
Together composing our joy and our pain.

In the warmth of your gaze, the world starts to fade,
A lullaby whispers, our fears it invades.
With hands held together, we craft our own song,
A melody sweet where we both can belong.

As night paints the canvas with colors anew,
The heartbeats in harmony guide us on through.
With every embrace, our spirits collide,
In love's gentle music, forever we bide.

Within the Labyrinth of Us

Tangled paths winding, where shadows reside,
In the labyrinth of us, our secrets collide.
Each turn brings a memory, cherished or lost,
The maps of our hearts drawn with passion's frost.

Through corridors echoing laughter and tears,
We search for the answers that melt all our fears.
In the depths of the maze, our truths intertwine,
As we navigate love, both fragile and divine.

With every wrong turn, we learn where to grow,
Beneath the starlit sky, we find our own flow.
The walls may be high, but our spirits are bold,
In this maze of devotion, our story unfolds.

Together we wander through night's gentle haze,
Finding solace and strength in love's winding ways.
For even in chaos, our hearts know the trust,
In the labyrinth of us, it's love that we must.

Echoes in the Dark

In the stillness of night, where whispers reside,
Echoes of longing bring shadows to guide.
The moon drapes her light on secrets we keep,
In the silence, our hearts dare to leap.

Through corridors empty, where silence can scream,
We chase the reflections of love's tender dream.
With every heartbeat, the darkness reveals,
The pulse of our souls, the truth that it feels.

In the depths of the dark, we find our own spark,
Illuminating paths that were hidden or stark.
Each echo a promise, a signal so clear,
In the shadows of night, your presence is near.

As dawn breaks the silence, we'll hold onto light,
Transforming the echoes that haunted the night.
For in every shadow, a story's embraced,
In the echoes of darkness, our love finds its place.

Undercurrents of Trust

Beneath the stillness, whispers flow,
Silent promises only we know.
In shadows deep, our truth aligns,
A bond unbroken, through endless times.

In glances shared, our stories breathe,
Each tender moment, our hearts wreathe.
Through storms and doubts, we find our way,
With every dawn, trust holds sway.

The currents strong, they pull and sway,
Yet in your eyes, I wish to stay.
Deep in the waters, fears may swim,
But together, love's light won't dim.

In quiet depths, we lay our fears,
Echoing laughter, shedding tears.
Hand in hand, we brave the tide,
In this dance, we'll always confide.

So let us cherish this sacred trust,
A treasure unscathed, pure and just.
Through every challenge and rise,
In the depths of love, the truest prize.

The Canvas of Us

On a canvas wide, our colors blend,
Each stroke tells tales that never end.
In vibrant hues, our dreams ignite,
With every brush, we chase the light.

From gentle whispers, we find our voice,
In the chaos, we learn to rejoice.
Splashes of laughter, shades of grace,
Together we paint, we find our place.

Every moment, a brush's dance,
In this gallery, we take our chance.
The palette rich, the shades profound,
In love's embrace, we are unbound.

With each new layer, our story grows,
In the depth of hues, our passion shows.
We share our dreams, we chase the stars,
In this masterpiece, there are no bars.

As time flows on, our canvas shines,
A work of art, forever defines.
In every heartbeat, in every sigh,
The canvas of us will never die.

Mirrors in the Abyss

In the dark, reflections gleam,
Fragments of thoughts, a shifting dream.
Faces change, yet souls remain,
In the mirror's depth, we dance through pain.

From shadows cast, our truths emerge,
In swirling depths, emotions surge.
A silent scream, a whispered plea,
Within the void, it's you and me.

These mirrors show what we can't see,
The hidden depths of you and me.
Behind each gaze, a story flows,
In the abyss, understanding grows.

As we dive deeper into night,
We find the spark, we seek the light.
In reflective waters, fears can swim,
But together we rise, we fight, we brim.

So fear not the depths, my dear friend,
In this abyss, our love won't end.
For in each mirror, we shine so bright,
Together, we conquer, together ignite.

Layers of Intimacy

Peeling back the layers, slow and sweet,
In every glance, our hearts compete.
Softly spoken, secrets shared,
In this dance, our souls are bared.

A touch here, a breath there,
Every moment, a silent prayer.
Skin on skin, we find our truth,
In the depths of love, we reclaim youth.

The layers fold like petals bloom,
In the quiet night, dispelling gloom.
Each heartbeat echoes, a silent song,
In this embrace, we both belong.

With every fold, we intertwine,
In this journey, our spirits shine.
Through whispered words, we break the mold,
In layers rich, our love unfolds.

So let us cherish this sacred space,
In every layer, we find grace.
With open hearts and hands entwined,
In intimacy's layers, forever aligned.

Unfurling Our Truths

In the quiet dawn, we speak,
Layers peel, the heart feels weak.
Words like petals touch the light,
Revealing shadows, pure and bright.

Embrace the flaws that lie within,
Every scar tells where we've been.
Truths once hidden, now unfold,
In tender hands, the dreams take hold.

Beneath the weight of whispered fears,
We find the strength through whispered tears.
Each confession, a gentle breeze,
Unlocking hearts, with fragile ease.

In unity, we rise and soar,
Together, braver than before.
Sunshine dances on the past,
With open arms, our love holds fast.

So let us stand with courage true,
In the light, for me and you.
Unfurling now, our spirits free,
A tapestry of you and me.

The Silent Symphony

In stillness, echoes softly play,
Notes uncharted, drift away.
Each heartbeat hums a quiet song,
A melody where we belong.

With every breath, the world retreats,
Harmony in quiet beats.
Lost in thoughts that rise and fall,
A symphony that speaks for all.

The whispers of the trees around,
Nature's music, pure and profound.
In silence, we begin to see,
How gentle rhythms set us free.

The stars above compose a line,
In shadows, secrets intertwine.
Within the hush, we find our way,
Embracing night, embracing day.

The silent symphony unfolds,
A tale of love, timeless and bold.
In quiet moments, we unite,
Creating beauty in the night.

Interwoven Paths

Two souls wandering, side by side,
Through winding ways, where dreams reside.
Fate has stitched our stories tight,
In the tapestry of day and night.

We've danced on edges, close to fears,
Shared laughter, joy, and countless tears.
With every step, our roots grow deep,
Entwined in moments, sacred keep.

The sun may set, yet we hold fast,
In shadows long, our bond will last.
Winding paths beneath the stars,
Together, healing every scar.

With open hearts, we face the tide,
In storms that rage, we will abide.
Each path we walk, a stride of grace,
In every turn, love's warm embrace.

Interwoven, forever we'll be,
A journey shared, you and me.
Through every challenge, we'll rise,
Together bound, beneath the skies.

Mapping Our Intimacy

With gentle strokes, we draw our maps,
Charts of laughter, love, perhaps.
Each line a memory, soft and sweet,
In corners where our hearts do meet.

Through winding streets of whispered dreams,
We trace with care, or so it seems.
In silken threads, we weave our tales,
A narrative where love prevails.

The landmarks mark our shared embrace,
In each glance, familiar grace.
With every star, a promise shines,
In the vast night, our heart's designs.

Together navigating this expanse,
In the silence, give love a chance.
In every heartbeat, we will find,
The depths of souls, so intertwined.

Mapping intimacy, hand in hand,
We cultivate this sacred land.
With every moment, we explore,
The boundless love we can't ignore.

Chasing the Horizon

With every step, the sky calls,
Endless dreams where the sun falls.
Colors blend in a soft embrace,
Hope ignites in this sacred space.

The winds whisper secrets untold,
Guiding hearts both young and old.
Running fast towards fading light,
Chasing shadows into the night.

Each sunrise brings a new chance,
To dance lightly, the world in trance.
Miles traverse, yet never tire,
With passion born of bright desire.

The ocean breathes a timeless sea,
Inviting souls to set them free.
Horizons stretch beyond our sight,
Life's journey bathed in golden light.

In the distance, dreams ignite,
Chasing warmth in the fading night.
With every heartbeat, we explore,
The vastness of what lies in store.

Reflections in the Tide

Waves dance softly on the shore,
Carrying whispers of days before.
Each ebb and flow tells a tale,
A soothing rhythm, a gentle sail.

Mirrored skies in ocean deep,
Secrets hidden, we must keep.
Footprints washed by the calming sea,
Moments drifting, just you and me.

Time stands still on shores of gold,
A treasure chest of dreams untold.
Reflections shimmer, faces concede,
In the water, we plant the seed.

With every crest, our hearts align,
In tides of trust, our souls entwine.
Moonlit paths guide us tonight,
Navigating through joys and fright.

In the quiet, let us find
The strength to leave the past behind.
In reflections, we learn to grow,
Finding peace in the gentle flow.

Untangling the Knots

Thoughts entwined like twisted string,
Anxious minds pull at everything.
Finding calm in a stormy sea,
Untangling what burdens me.

Each knot tells stories of the past,
Confusions weighed, shadows cast.
Step by step, unravel the thread,
Speaking truths that need to be said.

Patience whispers in the dark,
Finding light in every spark.
Breathe in peace, release the strife,
In the chaos, discover life.

Hands reach out, embrace the fray,
Together we'll find our way.
As we mend what's torn apart,
Strength emerges within the heart.

With each unravel, clarity grows,
In the stillness, the heart knows.
Knot by knot, we'll find our flight,
Transcending through the endless night.

The Language of Touch

In a world where silence speaks,
The softest bond is what we seek.
Fingers trace a tender line,
Whispers shared when hearts align.

A brush of skin, a fleeting glance,
Moments spark like a timeless dance.
Connection blooms, the air alive,
In every touch, we truly thrive.

Soft caress in twilight's glow,
Binding souls in warmth's gentle flow.
Electric pulses, hearts collide,
In that moment, there's no divide.

The language of touch, pure and sweet,
A silent promise, a rhythmic beat.
Words unspoken, yet understood,
In each caress, there lies a mood.

Together we weave a tapestry,
Crafting dreams in unity.
In the essence of touch, we find,
A world created, intertwined.

Whispers Beneath the Surface

In shadows deep, where secrets dwell,
The murmurs rise, a silent swell.
Beneath the calm, a current flows,
Whispers of dreams that no one knows.

Lost thoughts adrift on water's crest,
They dance and play, forever pressed.
In the twilight's glow, a glimpse of light,
Reveals the tales of day and night.

Each ripple holds a tender touch,
A language soft, it means so much.
With every wave, a story spun,
In stillness found, we are as one.

Through depths unseen, our hearts align,
In noise and hush, the stars will shine.
Connected souls in quiet spaces,
Where love endures, time gently traces.

So let us dive beneath the blue,
To find the whispers shared by two.
In every swell, in every sigh,
Together we shall learn to fly.

Tides of Connection

The moon's soft pull, a guiding force,
Draws hearts together, sets the course.
Like ocean waves that kiss the shore,
We ebb and flow, forevermore.

With every tide, our spirits rise,
In salty air, beneath blue skies.
Our laughter mingles with the breeze,
In moments shared, we find our ease.

As sunbeams dance on waters clear,
Each glimmer speaks, the world can hear.
The bonds we weave, a tapestry,
Of memories cherished, wild and free.

Each heartbeat syncs with nature's song,
In harmony where we belong.
The currents strong, they carry dreams,
In whispered hopes and silver gleams.

So sail these tides, with hearts in tune,
Embrace the magic morning's bloom.
In every wave, in every glow,
The tides of connection gently flow.

Echoes in Our Silence

In quietude, our hearts converse,
A language rich, the universe.
In hushed breaths shared beneath the stars,
We find the strength of who we are.

The stillness hums with memories near,
Whispers of joy, and drawn-out fear.
Yet in the void, there's space to grow,
In silence, love begins to show.

The world around can fade away,
Yet in our hearts, we'll always stay.
With tender glances, we're entwined,
In echoes soft, our souls aligned.

Each pause we take, a breath anew,
In tranquil moments, we break through.
Together here, we're truly free,
In echoes loud, we hear the sea.

So let the quiet hold us tight,
In shadows deep, we find the light.
In every silence, love's refrain,
Echoes linger, joy and pain.

Threads of Heartstrings

With every beat, a thread connects,
A tapestry of hopes, reflects.
In warmth of clasped hands, we weave,
The comfort found in what we believe.

Through vibrant hues of joy and strife,
The fabric holds the dance of life.
In moments shared, our spirits blend,
Each thread a tale, a cherished friend.

As seasons change, the patterns shift,
New colors born, a perfect gift.
Through trials faced, we gather strong,
In unity, we sing our song.

So let us tie these strands with care,
In every glance, in sweet despair.
For heartstrings plucked will always bind,
A melody of love entwined.

In every knot, a promise made,
With threads of trust that won't soon fade.
Together, woven in life's scheme,
We find our strength, our shared dream.

Souls Intertwined in Silence

In quiet nooks where shadows dwell,
Two souls whisper, secrets swell.
Fingers touch in gentle grace,
Finding solace in their space.

The world fades to a muted hue,
As silence sings the love so true.
Each heartbeat echoes, soft and clear,
A language only they can hear.

Moonlight dances on the floor,
Illuminating what's in store.
In stillness, hearts begin to blend,
A bond that knows no start or end.

Time suspends, and dreams take flight,
Wrapped in warmth, they own the night.
Every glance, a promise made,
In silence, fears dissolve and fade.

Together, they weave a tale,
Of whispered winds and soothing sail.
In the night, their hearts eclipse,
Souls intertwined in tranquil slips.

Submerged in Each Other

Beneath the waves, where colors glide,
Two hearts poise, side by side.
In a world both deep and wide,
They find the calm, they find the tide.

Submerged in depths, they intertwine,
Each breath, a rhythm, pure, divine.
Hands encircle, warmly clasp,
In ocean's embrace, love's sweet gasp.

Currents sway, but they hold fast,
With dreams of future, echoes of past.
Whispers echo through the blue,
In their depths, a love so true.

The sea may roar, but here they stay,
Lost in warmth, adrift, they play.
A refuge found beneath the light,
Submerged, they bloom, in endless night.

Together they drift, on gentle waves,
Where time is still, and love behaves.
Forever held in watery dance,
Submerged in each other's glance.

The Depths of Togetherness

In the dark, where secrets lie,
Two souls unite, a silent tie.
Deep waters churn with every breath,
In love, they find the dance of death.

Beneath the surface, warmth resides,
In the depths, no need for guides.
Every heartbeat, a steady tide,
In togetherness, they find their stride.

Through currents strong, they navigate,
In tangled waves, they celebrate.
Trust their compass, firm and bright,
In the depths, they take to flight.

With gentle waves, they greet the morn,
In each other, a new day born.
Submerged in love, they're never lost,
Together, they pay the quiet cost.

A voyage deep, through dark and light,
In each other's arms, everything feels right.
In the ocean's heart, they find their bliss,
The depths of togetherness, a perfect kiss.

Oceanic Bonds

The tides of fate, they ebb and flow,
With every touch, they gently grow.
In salty air, they breathe as one,
    Underneath a setting sun.

Waves crash, but they stand tall,
A love that answers nature's call.
In harmony, their spirits soar,
    Oceanic bonds forevermore.

Tangled together, like seaweed strands,
They drift through life, hand in hand.
With currents pulling, they won't stray,
In love's embrace, they find their way.

The ocean's song, a lullaby,
In liquid depths, their dreams fly high.
No storm can break what's woven tight,
    In oceanic bonds, hearts ignite.

Together they roam, from shore to shore,
With laughter shared, they long for more.
In salty kisses, time stands still,
    Oceanic bonds, a love to fill.

Ripples of Shared Moments

In the quiet glances we share,
Memories dance on the air,
Laughter echoes through the night,
Together we chase the light.

Hand in hand, we roam free,
Painting worlds for you and me,
Every whisper, every sigh,
Builds our story, soars high.

Time weaves moments, so dear,
Threads of joy, threads of fear,
Each heartbeat a sacred tune,
Underneath the silver moon.

In the tapestry we've spun,
All the shadows, all the fun,
Ripples spread with every smile,
Together, we'll travel each mile.

As we journey, let us find,
Every dream, intertwined,
In the echoes, let us dwell,
In these ripples, all is well.

Veins of Empathy

Through the cracks, compassion flows,
In the silence, kindness grows,
Hearts entwined, we deeply feel,
Whispers shared, a soothing seal.

Veins of empathy, we trace,
Finding solace in each space,
In the struggles, in the pain,
Unity binds us like a chain.

Every story, every tear,
Holding close what we hold dear,
In the darkness, light's rebirth,
Finding meaning in our worth.

From the ashes, hope will rise,
In each other's honest eyes,
Together, we break the mold,
Our shared strength, forever bold.

With each heartbeat, we ignite,
Empathy's glow, shining bright,
Hand in hand, we'll pave the way,
In our hearts, warmth will stay.

A Tale of Two Heartbeats

Two heartbeats in sync as one,
Beneath the vast, unyielding sun,
Whispers travel on the breeze,
Painting dreams among the trees.

Moments stitched with finest thread,
Through the journeys we've both tread,
Shared laughter, and stories old,
A tale of love, forever told.

In the rhythm of day and night,
In every shadow, in every light,
Two souls blazing, intertwined,
Discovering what it means to bind.

Through the storms, through the calm,
Finding peace in every psalm,
Together we rise, hand in hand,
Writing history, a cherished strand.

With each heartbeat, in the flow,
The pulse of life in gentle glow,
A tale of love, both fierce and sweet,
In the dance of life, we're complete.

Exploring the Unfathomable

Beneath the stars, we gaze wide,
In the cosmos, heartbeats glide,
Questions linger, mysteries call,
In the depths, we dare to fall.

Unraveling the threads of time,
Seeking answers, sensing rhyme,
In the shadows, light is found,
In the silence, truth resounds.

Across the oceans, vast and free,
Chasing dreams, just you and me,
With each step, horizons grow,
In the unknown, we learn to flow.

Curiosity's spark ignites,
In the darkness, shimmers lights,
Exploring realms beyond our sight,
Together, we chase the night.

As we wander, let us dare,
To embrace what's waiting there,
In our hearts, the universe,
Exploring all, we will immerse.

Shadows We Share

In the twilight, whispers fade,
Underneath the towering shade.
Footsteps linger, hearts entwined,
Secrets woven, souls aligned.

Flickering leaves, a gentle sigh,
Promises made beneath the sky.
Shadows dance, the night unfolds,
Stories shared, as time beholds.

In the silence, dreams take flight,
Casting echoes into the night.
Familiar paths where we both roam,
In every shadow, we find home.

Through the corridors of the past,
Memories cherished, forever cast.
Hand in hand, we face the dawn,
Together strong, forever drawn.

As the stars begin to gleam,
In our hearts, we hold a dream.
Together we'll chase the fall,
In shadows shared, we find it all.

Navigating the Unseen

In the depths where visions blind,
We seek the truths we wish to find.
Maps unwritten, trails unknown,
Guided by the seeds we've sown.

Through the mist, we take a leap,
In the silence, secrets keep.
Tides that pull, currents that sway,
Leading us through night and day.

Voices whisper, shadows call,
In the dark, we stand tall.
Unseen forces, guide our way,
As we dance on hopes' array.

With brave hearts, we chart our course,
Unraveling fate's silent force.
In the stillness, we will thrive,
Knowing in the unseen, we are alive.

Each turn taken, lessons learned,
In this journey, passion burned.
Navigating without a seam,
Together, we fulfill the dream.

Currents of Emotion

Rushing waters, deep and wide,
Feelings coursing, as they collide.
Tidal waves of joy and pain,
Carried forward, we remain.

In the stillness, memories flow,
Like a river, steady and slow.
Currents pulling, hearts at stake,
In the depths, our spirits wake.

Moments captured, laughter shared,
In the whirlpool, we are bared.
Trusting the waves, we plunge in deep,
From the surface, secrets seep.

Every drop a tale we weave,
In this dance, we learn to believe.
Floating free on this vast sea,
Currents of emotion, you and me.

As the dawn spills light anew,
In the waters, I find you.
Hand in hand, we ride the tide,
Together forever, side by side.

The Uncharted Waters

Beyond the map, horizons fade,
In the unknown, dreams cascade.
Waves of wonder call us near,
Into the depths, we shed our fear.

With every splash, a story grows,
In uncharted waters, adventure flows.
Sailing forth on faith's embrace,
Navigating time and space.

Stars above guide the way,
In the dark, we won't stray.
Charting paths with every breath,
In the journey, we find depth.

Voices echo through the spray,
As we drift, come what may.
In these waters, we belong,
Together we are brave and strong.

Every wave, a lesson learned,
In the fire of passion burned.
Through uncharted seas, we'll glide,
Together forever, side by side.

The Ocean Between Us

Waves crash with whispered sighs,
Salt air carries our goodbyes.
Miles stretch beneath the blue,
Yet my heart still beats for you.

Let the tide erase the pain,
Hold me close, like gentle rain.
Fading footprints in the sand,
Echo dreams we both had planned.

Stars above, a guiding light,
In the dark, we find our flight.
Every swell a lover's tune,
Together once, like sun and moon.

Depths conceal a secret song,
Two lost souls where we belong.
Beneath the waves, our hopes reside,
In the ocean wide and wide.

Through the storms and raging seas,
We will dance on autumn breeze.
Though the distance pulls apart,
You remain within my heart.

Beneath the Calm Surface

Hidden depths, silent dreams,
Underneath the quiet streams.
What lies deep, beneath the peace,
Hints of heartache, soft release.

Ripples dance with gentle grace,
Secrets held in water's embrace.
Sinking down where shadows dwell,
Whispers rise from the ocean's well.

Fingers trace the silken flow,
Gentle currents, ebb and grow.
In the depths, the truth is found,
Beneath the calm, a haunting sound.

Echoes of what once was real,
Floating softly, wounds to heal.
Beneath the calm, life interweaves,
The heart remembers, never leaves.

In the silence, fears take flight,
Lost in dreams, we seek the light.
Beneath the calm, a world so vast,
Finding peace in shadows past.

Heartstrings in the Deep

Tethered tight, our fates entwined,
In the depths, our hearts aligned.
Though the waters surge and rise,
I can see you in the skies.

Pulled by currents, fierce and bold,
Stories waiting to be told.
Each heartbeat a wave's embrace,
Drawing life from unknown space.

Through the dark, we wade and flow,
With every tide, our yearnings grow.
Strings of fate in rhythm play,
Guiding us, come what may.

In the silence, feelings surge,
Heartstrings tugging at the urge.
In the deep, I feel your fire,
With each pulse, desire grows higher.

Sailing on this sea so wide,
In your depths, I choose to abide.
Together bound, no need for light,
For in the dark, we shine so bright.

Fluid Dialogues

Words flow like water's grace,
In this dance, we find our place.
Gentle ripples, laughter shared,
In each moment, love declared.

Thoughts like tides that rise and fall,
Echo softly, a siren's call.
In the current, we will speak,
Finding solace, never weak.

Questions drift on flowing streams,
Seeking truths beyond our dreams.
In each wave, a story's spun,
Fluid dialogues, two as one.

Moments lost to time's embrace,
Together shared, we leave a trace.
Every glance, a word unsaid,
In the silence, love is bred.

As we float through life's vast sea,
Fluid dialogues set us free.
Hand in hand, we weave our song,
In this dance, where we belong.

Mapping Our Underwater World

Beneath the waves, a realm so vast,
Colors dance in shadows cast.
Coral gardens, life abounds,
Mysteries in silence found.

Bubbles rise, a gentle breeze,
Whispers carried through the seas.
Guiding stars in the ocean's night,
Charting depths of pure delight.

Fins and scales in harmony,
Nature's vibrant tapestry.
With each stroke, we mark the flow,
The secrets only currents know.

Echoes linger in the blue,
Stories waiting to ensue.
Weaving maps with every dive,
Unlocking worlds where dreams survive.

In depths where light begins to fade,
A journey into the cascade.
Unfolding wonders, a treasure trove,
In the heart of the ocean's grove.

The Weight of Words Unsaid

In silence rests the heavy heart,
Each thought, a fragile work of art.
Fingers tremble, lips stay still,
Yearning whispers, unfulfilled.

Moments lost in quiet night,
Shadows cast by fading light.
Promises hang upon the air,
Weight of words too much to bear.

Regret weaves through every dream,
As echoes fade in silent scream.
Thoughts collide in tangled threads,
In safety, voices tiptoe, tread.

Courage falters, hearts confine,
Wishing for a spark divine.
Yet hope flickers in the dark,
Awaiting still that kindling spark.

In time, the courage will arise,
To share the truths beneath the skies.
Unburdened now, we'll find our song,
And celebrate where we belong.

Unraveling Depths Together

In quiet moments, hands entwined,
We explore the depths of mind.
Like divers in a briny sea,
Unraveling what's meant to be.

Echoes of laughter guide our way,
Beneath the waves where shadows play.
With every question that we seek,
The ocean's truth begins to speak.

We dive into the unexplored,
Discover treasures, truths adored.
Secrets shared like whispers soft,
Floating higher, spirits aloft.

Beneath the surface, fears dissolve,
Together, we begin to solve.
In every current, we find grace,
Two souls united, time and space.

In waters deep, we're never alone,
Exploring realms that we have grown.
With every breath, we face the tide,
In this adventure, hearts collide.

Embracing the Unseen Currents

In hidden depths, the currents flow,
Whispers stir that few may know.
Beyond the shore, the wild winds sigh,
We venture forth, our spirits high.

Like sea glass caught in sunlit rays,
Our dreams unfold in vibrant ways.
We greet the storms, the unknown tide,
Together here, we will abide.

Embracing each unseen embrace,
We dance in rhythms, find our place.
With every wave that crashes near,
We gather strength, dismiss our fear.

In shadows cast, some beauty lies,
A journey shaped under dark skies.
For in the depths, we learn to see,
All that we are and can be free.

So let us trust the path we take,
Through currents fierce, our hearts won't break.
In unity, we'll brave the swell,
Together, our stories weave and tell.

The Space Between Hearts

In whispers soft, we seek the light,
Where shadows dance, and hearts take flight.
A breath away, yet worlds apart,
The silent bond, the beating heart.

Fingers trace the unseen line,
In moments lost, your soul is mine.
A touch of hope in every sigh,
In the quiet, love draws nigh.

Two souls that glide on fate's own wings,
In unison, the silence sings.
Between us lies a sacred space,
Where time stands still, and dreams embrace.

Though miles may stretch, and time may bend,
In every thought, you are my friend.
Through every storm and gentle breeze,
Our hearts will dance with perfect ease.

So let us hold what's deep inside,
In the space where love will bide.
For though apart, we'll never part,
Together, always, heart to heart.

Unspoken Promises

In glances shared, our secrets hide,
Beyond the words, where dreams confide.
A silent vow, a gentle glance,
In quiet moments, we find our chance.

These whispered thoughts, a tender thread,
A path unwalked, where fears have fled.
Our hearts entwined, though left unsaid,
In every smile, our truths are bred.

What lies between the lines we weave,
Is woven tight, we both believe.
A bond that time cannot erase,
In every heartbeat, a soft embrace.

Through storms that test, and light that shines,
We'll find our way, where love defines.
In shadows cast, we'll brave the night,
Our unspoken dreams, our guiding light.

Hold fast to hope and timeless grace,
In every moment, we find our place.
These promises, though unvoiced, we swear,
In the stillness, love lingers there.

Journey Through the Currents

With open hearts, we sail afar,
Through winding paths, beneath the stars.
The currents guide, the tides will sway,
In nature's arms, we find our way.

The waters churn, both wild and free,
With every wave, you're here with me.
Through tangled paths, we navigate,
Together strong, we face our fate.

Each twist and turn, a tale unfolds,
In every splash, new dreams behold.
The river sings a timeless song,
With every stroke, we both belong.

Where sunlight kisses deeper seas,
And every breeze brings sweet reprieves.
Through laughter, tears, in joy or strife,
We journey on, hand in hand, in life.

As stars align and currents shift,
We find our course, an endless gift.
To sail together, come what may,
In this adventure, love will stay.

Serenity in the Storm

The winds may howl, the thunder roar,
Yet in your eyes, I find the shore.
A calming peace amidst the fray,
Your presence holds the night at bay.

With every clash, our spirits rise,
In chaos found, we seek the skies.
A sanctuary, strong and warm,
We gather strength, a perfect balm.

When darkness looms, hold tight to me,
In raging storms, we'll find the sea.
Together, we'll withstand the fight,
Through restless days and endless night.

So let the tempests come and go,
In love, we find the strength to flow.
A gentle heart, a fierce embrace,
In every storm, we find our place.

After the rain, the sun will gleam,
In quiet moments, we'll dare to dream.
Through every trial, we'll feel the light,
For love endures, through darkest night.

In the Spaces Between

Whispers float in quiet air,
Moments linger, seldom shared.
Silent glances, hearts collide,
In the spaces where dreams abide.

Truths unspoken, shadows cast,
Fragments of a fleeting past.
Bated breath and racing hearts,
In the spaces, love imparts.

Time stands still, yet slips away,
In the night and in the day.
Hands that touch, but never grasp,
In the spaces where we clasp.

Echoes dance on paths unknown,
In the silence, seeds are sown.
Hope arises, fears disperse,
In the spaces, dreams immerse.

Life unfolds with every breath,
In the spaces, love outlasts death.
Eternity in fleeting time,
In the spaces, spirits climb.

The Depths of Knowing

In the shadows, wisdom lies,
Beneath the surface, truth defies.
Subtle currents weave the tale,
In the depths, we must not fail.

Questions linger in the void,
Seeking answers, rarely buoyed.
Heavy waters, fierce and deep,
In the depths, secrets keep.

A diver's heart, both brave and true,
Plunges down to seek what's due.
With every breath, we touch the core,
In the depths, we learn to soar.

Veils of doubt can cloud the way,
Yet the light will guide the stray.
Through the dark, we find our path,
In the depths, we face our wrath.

Knowledge blooms where courage stands,
In the depths, we understand.
Life's great ocean, vast and wide,
In the depths, we find our stride.

Twists of Fate

Life's a dance of chance and choice,
In the silence, you'll hear the voice.
Paths converge and then diverge,
In the twists, our dreams emerge.

Moments fleeting, yet profound,
In the chaos, hope is found.
Fortunes change, a fickle game,
In the twists, we fan the flame.

Every turn we didn't see,
Shapes our fate, sets us free.
Winds of fortune, strong and bold,
In the twists, our stories unfold.

Laughter lingers, tears may flow,
In the twists, our spirits grow.
Embrace the unknown, dare to wait,
In the twists, we navigate.

With every stumble, lessons learned,
In the twists, our hearts are burned.
Yet we rise, we learn to skate,
In the twists of our fate.

The Fire Beneath the Ice

Veiled in cold, a spark remains,
Beneath the frost, desire gains.
Silent passion, hidden deep,
The fire beneath, secrets keep.

Chilled winds may mask the flame,
Yet the warmth is never tamed.
Hearts collide in icy grace,
The fire beneath, we must embrace.

Frosted breath and longing sighs,
In the winter, passion lies.
From the stillness, embers glow,
The fire beneath begins to show.

In the quiet, feelings bloom,
Whispers from the heart's own room.
Through the layers, heat will rise,
The fire beneath defies the skies.

Embers spark in frozen night,
In the dark, we find our light.
As seasons change, ice will melt,
The fire beneath our hearts is felt.

Beyond the Surface

Beneath the waves, the secrets dwell,
In shadows where the stories swell.
A glimmer caught in muted light,
Echoes of dreams that take flight.

Waves crash softly on the shore,
Whispers of ages, tales of lore.
Beneath the tides, a world untold,
Mysteries waiting to unfold.

The ocean's breath, a soothing balm,
In turbulent times, it's always calm.
Each crest and trough, a dance of fate,
In silence, we learn to wait.

Flashes of truth in foam and spray,
Life teaches lessons in its own way.
Yet still we dive, beyond the veil,
In depths of wonder, we prevail.

So take a plunge, let go of fear,
Beyond the surface, magic is near.
With every stroke, we find our place,
In the embrace of nature's grace.

Frozen in the Moment

Time stands still beneath the snow,
In crystal silence, dreams can grow.
Each flake a whisper, soft and light,
A dance of winter, pure and bright.

The world adorned in shimmering white,
A canvas blank, a pure delight.
Footsteps echo on the frozen ground,
In quiet stillness, joy is found.

Nature's breath, a frozen sigh,
Underneath the vast and gentle sky.
Moments captured, fleeting and rare,
In the chill, we feel the air.

Hearts entwined by the fireside glow,
Wrapped in blankets, warmth we know.
The rhythm of laughter fills the space,
In every glance, a warm embrace.

So let us treasure this frozen day,
While light and shadows dance and play.
For in this moment, all is right,
Together we sparkle, in winter's light.

Journeying Through Storms

Clouds gather fast, the winds arise,
A tempest brews beneath dark skies.
But hearts are strong, we won't despair,
In unity, we find our care.

With every wave that crashes down,
We'll wear the storm as our brave crown.
Fierce the gusts that test our will,
Yet in the struggle, we stand still.

Lightning flashes, the thunder roars,
We sail on seas with unseen shores.
For every challenge makes us grow,
In shared resilience, hope will flow.

So onward through the tempest's might,
We seek the calm, we search for light.
Together we face what lies ahead,
With every heartbeat, no fear to tread.

In glory found within the strife,
We journey forth, embracing life.
Through storms we sail, our spirits high,
In the darkest nights, we learn to fly.

The Unveiling

In veils of mist, the truth will gleam,
A reality birthed from a dream.
With patient hands, the layers peel,
The hidden wonders soon reveal.

A tapestry woven with time and care,
Stories of hopes, joys, and despair.
Like petals opening in the sun,
Each revelation, a journey begun.

Whispers float on the gentle breeze,
In every echo, we find our keys.
Secrets unfold, like pages turned,
In every glimpse, our spirits yearn.

As dawn breaks wide, the shadows fade,
In the light of truth, we're unafraid.
An unveiling tender, yet so bold,
In understanding, we break the mold.

Let hearts be open, eyes embrace,
In the unveiling, we find our place.
A world renewed, a beautiful sign,
Our souls entwined, in light we shine.

The Poetry of Togetherness

In the garden where we grow,
Hands entwined, hearts aglow.
Whispers dance on the breeze,
A symphony of silent pleas.

Each moment shared, a gentle thread,
Weaving kindness where words are said.
Side by side, we face the dawn,
In the light, our fears are gone.

Together we laugh, together we cry,
In the tapestry of life, you and I.
Every struggle, we breathe as one,
A journey taken, a race well run.

With every heartbeat, our spirits soar,
Building memories, we yearn for more.
In the shadows, we stand tall,
In the poetry of togetherness, we find our all.

As seasons change, we hold on tight,
Finding solace in shared delight.
Through the storms and sunny skies,
Our bond endures, and never dies.

The Fragile Balance

On the edge of time we teeter,
Life's a dance, a fragile meter.
Each choice a step upon the line,
Balancing dreams with the divine.

In shadows cast by noon's soft glow,
We find the strength we must bestow.
With gentle care, we tend the flame,
For in this balance, we earn our name.

Moments fleeting, like grains of sand,
We grasp what we can, with trembling hand.
Yet in the chaos, beauty remains,
An artful life, through joy and pains.

As we navigate the highs and lows,
Each stumble teaches us what grows.
In unity, we face the night,
Finding courage in shared light.

In every heartbeat, hear love's call,
Together we rise, together we fall.
In this fragile dance, we find our way,
The balance held in each new day.

Silent Conversations

In silence shared, a glance conveys,
A world of thoughts in gentle ways.
No words are needed, hearts align,
In the stillness, love's design.

Each heartbeat speaks what lips can't say,
In shadows where our souls play.
Through every pause, an unspoken bond,
A language felt, yet never donned.

The echo of footsteps through the hall,
A whispered promise, weaves a thrall.
Moments linger in the quiet air,
In silent conversations, we both care.

Together we watch the stars ignite,
In the velvet sky, a shared delight.
Time slips softly, yet we remain,
In the space between, there's no pain.

With every smile that lights the dark,
A universe ignites a spark.
In the realm of hearts that beat as one,
Silent conversations have begun.

Resilience in the Depths

In depths where shadows softly creep,
Resilience stirs, refusing sleep.
Through trials faced, we learn to fight,
Emerging stronger from the night.

In silence bound, we seek the light,
With every struggle, hearts ignite.
The weight of dreams may bend the spine,
But hope remains, a lifeline.

With every tear that falls like rain,
We gather strength to rise again.
In the dark, we find our grace,
A testament of time and place.

In whispered prayers and gentle sighs,
We breathe resilience, our spirits rise.
No storm too fierce to bear the fight,
In depths profound, we find our light.

With roots that dig deep, we grow and bloom,
Defying fate, dispelling gloom.
For in the depths, where shadows dwell,
Resilience sings, and we are well.

The Colors of Us

In fields of gold, we stand the same,
With hearts ablaze, we play the game.
Your laughter shines, a vibrant hue,
Together painted, me and you.

Through shades of blue and whispers light,
We weave our dreams both day and night.
In twilight's glow, we find our way,
A canvas bright, where colors play.

Emerald greens in summer's embrace,
A dance of joy, a warm heart's space.
As seasons change, our palette grows,
With every step, our story flows.

In deep maroons of autumn's tease,
We brush away the winter's freeze.
The colors blend, our tales entwined,
In artful strokes, our souls aligned.

So here we are, in hues so bold,
A tapestry of love, behold.
In every shade, our spirits rise,
A masterpiece beneath the skies.

When Leaves Fall Together

As golden leaves drift down the trees,
We share our whispers with the breeze.
Each autumn sigh sings sweet and low,
A dance of time, as soft winds blow.

In orange sunsets, shadows play,
Our hands entwined on this cool day.
Together roaming pathways bold,
With every step, sweet stories told.

The crunching sound beneath our feet,
A joyful rhythm, bittersweet.
For in this moment, hearts align,
As colors fade, our souls combine.

A tapestry of fall we weave,
With every leaf, we dare believe.
In nature's arms, love softly glows,
As winter nears, our bond just grows.

So let us lie where petals fall,
In whispered secrets, hear our call.
Together, facing days anew,
When leaves fall down, I'll fall with you.

Footprints on the Sand

In twilight's hush, where waves embrace,
We walked along, with gentle grace.
The shoreline whispered tales of old,
Our footprints left in grains of gold.

Each step we took, like time stood still,
The ocean's song, a soothing thrill.
With every tide, our dreams unfold,
A journey rich, like stories told.

The sun dipped low, a fiery dance,
In that soft light, we found romance.
Two hearts aligned, with dreams so grand,
Etched in love, like prints in sand.

As sea foam kissed the twilight shore,
Our laughter echoed evermore.
A moment shared, where time can bend,
In every wave, our love will blend.

So let us walk, through night and day,
For every tide will not betray.
In shifting sands, our story's cast,
In every footprint, love will last.

Symphony of Two Souls

In silken night, when stars align,
Our hearts compose a sweet design.
A symphony of whispered dreams,
Where love flows deep, or so it seems.

With every note, our spirits soar,
The echoes dance, forevermore.
In harmony, our souls entwined,
A melody of hearts combined.

The gentle rhythm of your sigh,
A tender tune, a soft reply.
We dance beneath the moonlit glow,
As every heartbeat starts to flow.

In this grand waltz, we find our way,
Through ups and downs, come what may.
Each chord we strike, a passion's flame,
Together playing love's sweet game.

So let us sing, just me and you,
In every note, our love rings true.
A symphony of two souls bright,
In endless music through the night.

Waves of Shared Laughter

Laughter spills like ocean tides,
Bringing joy that never hides.
Friends gather near, hearts aglow,
Moments cherished, time moves slow.

Echoes dance in sandy shores,
Memories made, a love that soars.
In every wave, a story told,
An endless treasure, pure as gold.

Together we chase the setting sun,
In every heartbeat, we are one.
Shared secrets whisper, soft and clear,
In this laughter, nothing to fear.

Life's storms may come, but we stand tall,
With laughter, we conquer it all.
Through tides of change, we hold on tight,
Creating magic in the night.

Each wave a symbol of love's embrace,
In shared laughter, we find our place.
Forever woven in time's great dance,
In every smile, we take a chance.

Chasing Shadows

In the twilight's gentle glow,
We dance where shadows softly flow.
Fleeting forms that fade away,
Chasing whispers of yesterday.

Through alleys dark, we weave and wind,
In shadows, secrets intertwined.
Echoes linger of dreams we sought,
In each dark corner, lessons taught.

The moonlight glimmers on our path,
Guiding us through the aftermath.
We dive into the unknown night,
Finding solace in the fading light.

With every step, our fears subside,
In shadows, we choose to confide.
Through hidden depths, our hearts ignite,
Together we vanish into the night.

In chasing shadows, we find our grace,
Mystery woven, a sacred space.
Hand in hand, two souls, one goal,
In this dance, we become whole.

Heartbeats in Time

In the rhythm of hearts, we sway,
Lost in the music, come what may.
Each beat a story, softly chime,
Echoing moments, heartbeats in time.

Through valleys deep, our dreams take flight,
In every heartbeat, pure delight.
Time may pass, yet we remain,
Bound by love, through joy and pain.

Whispers of hope in every glance,
Together we weave a timeless dance.
In soft embraces, we find our peace,
With every heartbeat, sweet release.

Seasons change, yet love holds fast,
Moments cherished, never surpassed.
Heartbeats echo in sync with night,
Guiding us under the stars so bright.

With every second, our souls entwine,
In this vast universe, you're forever mine.
A melody played through the sands of time,
In each heartbeat, our love will climb.

The Heart's Compass

In stillness found beneath the sky,
The heart whispers, never shy.
A compass forged in love's warm glow,
Guiding us where we long to go.

Through storms and trials, it leads the way,
In every moment, come what may.
With every pulse, a path unfolds,
Stories of courage and dreams retold.

Across vast oceans, through mountains high,
The heart's compass will always try.
To steer us through the shadows cast,
Finding light in memories past.

Trust the journey, embrace the quest,
In love's embrace, we find our rest.
With every beat, we chart our course,
Guided by this unwavering force.

In the quiet moments, listen near,
The heart's compass is always clear.
With love as our guide, we face the dawn,
Together forever, our spirits drawn.

In the Quiet of Our Depths

In shadows deep, where secrets dwell,
Whispers float, in silent spell.
Hearts entwined, yet worlds apart,
In the quiet, we find our heart.

Beneath the calm, the storms reside,
Echoes linger, the truth we hide.
In stillness, feelings start to rise,
Reflections glow, in hidden skies.

Through layers thick, we seek a way,
To touch the light, to greet the day.
In depths we wander, lost yet found,
In quiet moments, love resounds.

Each heartbeat soft, a muted drum,
In silence, there is peace to come.
Together we brave the silent night,
In the stillness, hearts take flight.

So let us delve, no fear of pain,
In the quiet, love will reign.
Through every dark, a spark will gleam,
In our depths, we weave a dream.

Surfaces and Underlinings

Beneath the light, a world concealed,
In shadows cast, truths revealed.
The surface gleams, yet underneath,
Lies a dance of heart and breath.

Color clashes, patterns play,
Stories told in a vibrant array.
Yet whispers murmur beneath the skin,
In every glance, a tale begins.

We hide our fears with painted smiles,
Yet ache for warmth across the miles.
Underneath the laughter's veil,
Wounds may heal, but scars prevail.

Through every glance, a message flows,
In depths of eyes, emotion grows.
Surfaces glisten, but the heart knows,
What lies beneath, it ever shows.

In every touch, a story's spun,
Of surfaces danced and battles won.
We thread the needle, love entwined,
In the spaces where hearts align.

The Language of Waves

The ocean speaks in rhythmic tones,
A gentle pulse, where beauty roams.
Each wave a whisper, soft and true,
In the language shared by me and you.

Cascading dreams upon the shore,
With every crash, we yearn for more.
Tides that rise and fall with grace,
In their rhythm, we find our place.

Seagulls cry, a song on high,
Carried by winds that kiss the sky.
In salty air, our worries cease,
In waves we find our wish for peace.

The ocean's heart beats wild and free,
It teaches us what it means to be.
A symphony of depths and light,
In waves we find our souls take flight.

So let us dance upon the tide,
With love as vast as the ocean wide.
Through every ebb, our spirits wave,
In the language of the sea, we crave.

Fractals of Emotion

In tangled shapes, our feelings grow,
A maze of hearts in softest glow.
Each curve a story, a turn of fate,
In fractals, love begins to resonate.

Patterns form in life's design,
Echoes of joy, and traces of pine.
Infinite paths that twist and blend,
In every corner, a message penned.

Layers deep, we strive to see,
The beauty wrapped in complexity.
A dance of chaos, wild and bold,
In fractals of emotion, truth unfolds.

Through fractal lenses, we perceive,
The parts that heart and mind achieve.
In every angle, a piece of us,
In the spiral's grace, we learn to trust.

So let us wander through this maze,
In every turn, a spark ablaze.
In fractals shared, we find the wide,
The depth of love, our hearts' true guide.

Soft Edges of Commitment

In whispered tones, we vow and grow,
With gentle hearts, our love will flow.
Through storms and calms, we'll stand as one,
In soft embrace, new days begun.

With each small step, we nurture trust,
In laughter bright, in shadows just.
Together strong, we'll face the night,
In every challenge, find our light.

Threads of promise weave our fate,
In honest words, we celebrate.
The dreams we share, like stars align,
In tender moments, love divine.

Soft edges paint our journey true,
With every glance, I see in you.
A world that blooms, for us to make,
In every heartbeat, love awake.

Through every trial, hand in hand,
We'll write our story, bold and grand.
With soft edges, hearts entwined,
In the canvas of our minds.

Threads in the Weave

In myriad colors, threads entwine,
Each story shared, a hand in mine.
Through laughter's echo, tears that bind,
We stitch the fabric of the kind.

With gentle care, we cross each seam,
Constructing life from dreams we dream.
The patterns form, our hearts align,
As time reveals the grand design.

In every knot, a lesson learned,
Through joys and grief, our spirits burned.
The tapestry of us unfolds,
In threads of warmth, our love retold.

We gather strands of life's embrace,
With every challenge, we find grace.
Our fingers dance, a skilled ballet,
In threads of hope, we find our way.

Together strong, as fibers twine,
We'll weave a tale, your heart in mine.
Through every twist, each chance we take,
In this grand weave, awake, awake.

Through the Lens of Love

With every glance, the world expands,
In vibrant hues, your heart demands.
Through every moment, time stands still,
In frames we capture, dreams fulfill.

The lens reveals what words can't say,
In silent whispers, love's ballet.
From echoes past, to futures bright,
Each snapshot glows, a shared delight.

In shadows cast, in light's embrace,
Your smile transforms this sacred space.
Through countless visions, we find our way,
In every click, love's sweet ballet.

The story unfolds, a film divine,
With memories rich, our hearts entwine.
Through laughter's lens and sorrow's tears,
We capture life throughout the years.

Through every angle, life's embrace,
With you, the world is a wondrous place.
In love's true focus, we shall see,
Through every lens, it's you and me.

Moonlight on Our Journey

Beneath the glow of the silvered moon,
Our hearts embark, a timeless tune.
With every step, the night ignites,
In whispered dreams, our love takes flight.

The shadows dance, a soft caress,
In moonlit paths, we find our rest.
With every heartbeat, stars align,
In gentle breezes, love's design.

Through winding trails, our spirits soar,
In nocturnal grace, we yearn for more.
Each moment shared, a treasure found,
In silvery light, our souls unbound.

As time unfolds, the night will fade,
But in our hearts, the memories laid.
With moonlight guiding, we'll never part,
For in this journey, you are my heart.

With every shimmer, hope shall rise,
In the embrace of starry skies.
Together always, through night and day,
In moonlight's glow, come what may.

The Currents We Create

In whispers soft, the waters sway,
We build our dreams, come what may.
A dance of tides, a gentle push,
Together we rise, in the evening hush.

The ripples spread, our laughter glows,
With every heartbeat, a current flows.
We shape the waves with every choice,
In harmony, we find our voice.

From quiet streams to oceans wide,
The paths we forge, the paths we bide.
In the depths of night, our hopes ignite,
Guided by stars, we chase the light.

Through storms that come, we stand as one,
An unbroken bond, till the day is done.
With every swell, we grow and change,
Embracing life, both wild and strange.

So let us sail where dreams abide,
Through currents fierce, and gentle tide.
For in our hearts, we hold the key,
To navigate life's vast, blue sea.

Reflections in a Sea of Hearts

In every gaze, a story spun,
Reflections dance, two souls as one.
A tempest brews, yet calm we stay,
In this vast sea, come what may.

With every pulse, the waters quake,
Hearts align, the choice we make.
In depths unknown, we seek the spark,
With whispered dreams that light the dark.

As tides recede, our truths emerge,
In silence deep, we feel the urge.
To dive within, to brave the storm,
In this embrace, our spirits warm.

With shimmering waves and shores of gold,
The tales of love will always be told.
For in this sea, our hearts take flight,
Together we weave, both day and night.

So let the currents guide us through,
In every heartbeat, I find you.
Reflections clear, our paths align,
In this sea of hearts, forever shine.

Navigating the Unseen

In shadows deep, we seek the light,
Through winding paths, in silent flight.
Each whispered thought, a guiding star,
Together we venture, near and far.

With every step, the fog reveals,
The truth we chase, the love that heals.
In hidden groves, our dreams reside,
Navigating life, heart open wide.

In moments lost, we find our way,
Through twists and turns, come what may.
With gentle hands, we chart the course,
In unity, we tap the source.

The unseen threads that bind us tight,
Illuminate the darkest night.
With trust as our compass, we will glide,
Across the waves, with hearts as guide.

So let us wander into the unknown,
With every breath, our courage grown.
In this dance of life, we are free,
Together navigating what's meant to be.

The Abyss of Hidden Feelings

In silence deep, emotions swell,
A tidal wave, a secret well.
The heart conceals what eyes can't see,
In shadows cast, we yearn to be.

With every sigh, the depths we face,
A labyrinth of dreams we trace.
In whispers low, the truth takes form,
A gentle ache, a quiet storm.

Beneath the surface, currents churn,
Yearning hearts, for love we yearn.
In hidden depths, our hopes reside,
In the abyss, we seek to hide.

Yet with each breath, the courage grows,
To share the pain, the love that flows.
In unison, we brave the night,
In vulnerability, we find our light.

So let us dive where feelings reign,
Embrace the joy, and face the pain.
For in this abyss, we rise and mend,
Together as one, till the very end.

Milton Keynes UK
Ingram Content Group UK Ltd.
UKHW022005131124
451149UK00013B/1010